COVENANTMeditations

COVENANT

Meditations

Nashville

COVENANT BIBLE STUDY
COVENANT MEDITATIONS

ISBN 978-1-4267-7220-7

These meditations were written by Pam Hawkins, one of the editors for Covenant Bible Study, a twenty-
four-week, in-depth study of the whole Bible.

Scripture quotations are from the Common English Bible. Copyright © 2011 by the Common English
Bible. All rights reserved. Used by permission. www.CommonEnglishBible.com.

Printed in China

14 15 16 17 18 19 20 21 22 23—10 9 8 7 6 5 4 3 2 1

Covenant Bible Study resources include:

Creating the Covenant: Participant Guide, ISBN 978-1-4267-7216-0
Living the Covenant: Participant Guide, ISBN 978-1-4267-7217-7
Trusting the Covenant: Participant Guide, ISBN 978-1-4267-7218-4
Covenant Bible Study App: Participant Guides for iOS and Android, ISBN 978-1-4267-7219-1

Covenant Bible Study: Covenant Meditations, ISBN 978-1-4267-7220-7
Covenant Bible Study: Covenant Meditations ePub, ISBN 978-1-4267-7221-4
Covenant Bible Study App: Covenant Meditations for iOS and Android, ISBN 978-1-4267-7222-1

Covenant Bible Study: Leader Guide, ISBN 978-1-4267-7223-8
Covenant Bible Study: Leader Guide eBook for eReaders, ISBN 978-1-4267-7225-2
Covenant Bible Study App: Leader Guide for iOS and Android, ISBN 978-1-4267-7224-5

Covenant Bible Study: DVD Video (set of three), ISBN 978-1-4267-8678-5
Covenant Bible Study: MP4 Video Episodes (download individually from CovenantBibleStudy.com)

CEB Study Bible, hardcover ISBN 978-1-6092-6028-6, decotone ISBN 978-1-6092-6040-8

To order resources or to obtain additional information for participants, Covenant groups, and leaders, go
to www.CovenantBibleStudy.com or to www.cokesbury.com. All print resources are available exclusively
from these online sites, from Cokesbury reps, or by calling Cokesbury (800-672-1789). The Covenant
Bible Study digital app is available from iTunes and Google Play.

Contents

Contents (Cont'd)

Praying the Scriptures

The LORD is my shepherd.
I lack nothing.
Psalm 23:1

Long before I learned about the words from Psalm 23—where they came from, whom they were for, how they were sung—I prayed them. I prayed them before I was in first grade. I prayed them sitting in the backseat of the family Pontiac on the way home from church. I prayed them as I colored the Sunday school picture of a young shepherd carrying a lost sheep on his shoulders. I neither knew that I was praying nor that my faith was being shaped as the words made a home in me while I colored, rode, and memorized. But now, many years later, I know that these scriptures, and many others, have given form, direction, and room for the prayers of my life, in much the same way that a creek bed holds and guides water from one place to another, while the water also changes and shapes the soil that holds it.

But somewhere along the way of faith and growing up, I got the idea that unless I understood scripture and knew its history, its location in the Bible, and the number of chapters and verses, my knowledge of scripture was incomplete and inadequate. I thought that the Bible was for "knowing" and "knowing about something."

Of course, Bible study is the best way to become proficient in God's word, which is a goal for any faithful child of the church. So along with others in my faith community, I began what is still a love affair with scripture. I studied the context, content, stories, royal records, literary forms, and theological texture of this holy book. In fact, I grew in confidence and knowledge about the meaning and life-changing power of the Bible's words.

Yet, for all the knowledge and insight obtained from years of study, the early formative prayers from my first encounters with God's word continue to resonate deep within my heart. These words, when prayed, seem to fit my life at the very times I need them most, whether or not I "know" or recall anything about them. I pray spontaneously, "The LORD is my shepherd. I lack nothing" (Ps 23:1). Or when things happen outside my control, "Don't be afraid" (Luke 1:30*a*). Or when life is racing down a gorge filled with boulders, "When you pass through the waters, I will be with you; when through the rivers, they won't sweep over you" (Isa 43:2*a*). There are days when I long to be watched over and tenderly shepherded. There are times when fear grips my heart, or when I feel as though I can barely tread the waters of my work, family, and life. And often, when nothing else seems to get through to me, the words of scripture flood my innermost parts, where God has "knit me together" (Ps 139:13*b*). And I am in prayer, again, guided and shaped by God's word.

> In the beginning was the Word
> > and the Word was with God
> > and the Word was God.
> The Word was with God in the beginning.
> Everything came into being through the Word,
> > and without the Word
> > nothing came into being.

John 1:1-3

As long as God's people have studied scripture, indeed, even longer, we have lived with God's Word as the source that lights the center of our lives. Our prayers, our days, our very existence wouldn't be in the world if not for the Word. Our earliest communication and communion with God is through the Word. Therefore, not only do we grow in faith by shining a light on scripture to learn about it, we also grow in faith by letting scripture shine a light on us—on who we are as people of God—on our hopes, needs, fears, intercessions, and longings. In other words, we grow in faith by letting scripture shine a light on the prayers of our lives.

This book of meditations is designed for the prayers of our lives. It is designed to help us engage God's holy word through prayer. In the pages that follow, one scripture passage from each book of the Bible is paired with a simple guide to pray that scripture. Based upon the ancient, classic tradition of praying the scriptures, the intention of this book is to offer readers an alternative approach to learning scripture—an approach where, if only for a little while, learning *from* scripture takes precedence over learning *about* scripture.

Through the spiritual practice of praying the scriptures, it is possible that our perspectives on reading the Bible might change a little, or even be transformed. Perhaps through the lens of prayer, rather than the lens of study, our eyes may refocus, giving us "eyes to see" more of what Jesus longs for us to see (see Mark 8:18). Many benefits come from reading scripture with our rational minds. Yet we can't know, unless we try, the full benefits that come from learning to pray scripture with our hearts. Try something new in prayer through God's word. It will change your heart and mind.

How to use *Covenant Meditations*

This book of meditations is designed for multiple uses.

1. It is a set of sixty-six meditations to expand or further develop the practice of praying scripture by participants in any in-depth Bible study. This guide is also aligned with Covenant Bible Study, an in-depth study of the whole Bible that convenes over a period of twenty-four weeks.

COVENANTMeditations

2. It is a prayer book for personal daily devotion that can be used by people of any age—young adults, youth, lay leaders, senior adults, friends, and pastors.

3. It can also be used by congregations that commit to praying through the Bible together, taking one book and one prayer at a time.

The scriptures and guidance for prayers are provided in this book, with space for making notes, drawing, or journaling. Each person has room for individual expression, but there is also space to record group comments if desired.

Covenant Bible Study Participants: Sixty-six scripture passages and sixty-six guides to prayer are contained in this resource. Readers should center on one scripture and prayer each week, taking time to live with the text and the prayer over several days, rather than pressing through a reading and prayer guide each day. But the pace and the timing of praying the scriptures are personal, and the right rhythm must be chosen by the reader or group. There is no right or wrong pace for this spiritual practice. But because we are so prone to "complete" work in other parts of our lives, if using this prayer book can help to cultivate a slowed-down, meditative practice of engaging God's word through prayer, it will be all the better.

To begin using this book, simply choose the portion of the day when you can set aside at least fifteen minutes for reading and prayer. This may be early in the morning, at midday, or right before bedtime. It doesn't matter which time you choose. It's more important that you find a time when there are few distractions for you. Some find it helpful to go to the same place each time for reading and praying, so that the location, lighting, and position in which you read become part of the experience. But most of all, be comfortable.

All you will need is your copy of *Covenant Meditations* and a pencil or pen. If you like to journal in a separate book, you may want to have that with you as well, but there is room on each page of *Covenant Meditations* to journal and make notes.

When you are ready, turn to page 15, where a text from the book of Genesis can be found. Slowly read the scripture passage and then, after a first reading, read the guide to prayer that follows the scripture. Each scripture reading has a different guide to prayer, so you will simply follow the instructions there for a specific way of praying the scriptures. Take the time you need, make the notes you wish to make, and pray the prayers that come to you. That is all you need to do.

Again, if you can, allow yourself to return to the same reading and prayer for one week. Stay with one book of the Bible for those seven days so that you can experience the different ways God may engage you through one reading at a time. Then, the next week, do the same for the scripture reading and guide to prayer for the book of Exodus. Follow this same pattern of reading and prayer through all sixty-six books.

A Companion for Spiritual Friends: If you and a friend decide to use this book together, agree on when you will begin your readings and prayers so that you are on the same schedule. Then find one time each week to be in touch with each other. This can be done in person, by phone, by e-mail, or online. Any personal connection will do. Spend time sharing the insights, questions, and prayers that have arisen from the scriptures and the prayer guides. Ask how you can support each other in your prayers, and write in your book the specific prayer requests that you share in your conversations.

A Resource for Small Groups: If you are part of a small group that wishes to use this book as its resource, begin with an organizational session in which everyone has a copy of *Covenant Meditations*. During this session, you can review the book and agree upon a rhythm of reading before your group gets started. Plan to meet once a week and for group sessions to last for one hour. Although it would be good if the group could meet for sixty-six weeks, it may be that the group wants to set a shorter time to gather, which will still provide time for a shared practice of praying the scriptures. Group members need to determine how many weeks they want to spend together using *Covenant Meditations* as a resource.

Each group member will need a copy of *Covenant Meditations* and will want to bring a pen or pencil to each group session. Some may want to use a journal in addition to the writing space provided for each reading. In preparation for each session, group members are asked to read the assigned scripture and follow the guide to prayer for that scripture beforehand. A daily reading and prayer schedule is a good goal for members to set, but each person will develop a personal practice and schedule.

When members gather for the initial group session, first spend time greeting each other and settling in. Then have two different group members read the assigned scripture, leaving a few moments of silence in between. Next, spend time sharing reactions and responses to the scripture reading. A question to prompt this reflection time might be: "What did you hear in this reading?" After ten minutes of conversation, move to a time of prayer, asking one group member to read aloud the guide to prayer for the assigned scripture. Then invite group members to share any insights, questions, prayers, or reflections from the experience of praying scripture. This provides a time and a setting to grow in prayer and to reflect on God's word. Each group will develop its own format, but be sure there is time for any group members who want to share. When the hour is almost complete, leave time for a closing prayer that group members take turns leading.

A Guide for Congregational Prayer: A congregation might want to spend sixty-six weeks (or a year) praying through the Bible by using *Covenant Meditations* as their prayer book for that season. Each participating member will need their own copy of the book, or families may prefer to share one book to be used in the home. A reading and prayer schedule will need to be communicated to the congregation through newsletters, worship announcements, websites, or social media announcements so that members of the congregation can be on the same schedule. A simple description of the plan and schedule will need to be shared throughout the sixty-six weeks so that people who come into the congregation after the readings and prayers have begun can easily join in.

Some attention will need to be given to the readings and prayers for each week. This can be accomplished in worship, in a weekly newsletter or website posting, on a bulletin board, at a midweek dinner, or via other congregational access points. Each congregation will determine what is best, but each will need some way in which to encourage and support ongoing participation and reflection. A congregational celebration might be planned at the end of praying the scriptures together.

Genesis

World's creation

When God began to create the heavens and the earth—the earth was without shape or form, it was dark over the deep sea, and God's wind swept over the waters—God said, "Let there be light." And so light appeared. God saw how good the light was. God separated the light from the darkness. God named the light Day and the darkness Night.

There was evening and there was morning: the first day.

Genesis 1:1-5

Praying the word

Silently read the passage from Genesis, paying attention to each word and phrase. Pause for a moment of quiet, and then read it again, this time using your imagination about the appearance of light on the first day of creation. What color is the light? How does it appear? What does it reveal? Offer a prayer for a person or circumstance you know about where God's good light is needed this day.

Exodus

God's special name

But Moses said to God, "If I now come to the Israelites and say to them, 'The God of your ancestors has sent me to you,' they are going to ask me, 'What's this God's name?' What am I supposed to say to them?"

God said to Moses, "I Am Who I Am. So say to the Israelites, 'I Am has sent me to you.'"

Exodus 3:13-14

Praying the word

God's name is revealed to Moses. Throughout scripture, our God is a God of many names: I Am, Lord, Father (*Abba*), shepherd, Jesus Christ, Spirit, wind, savior, rock, and more. In different seasons and at different times, God meets us in our needs, where we are. What name for God speaks to you today? Take your time with this question. Once you have chosen one of God's names that has meaning for you, write a prayer to God using this name, and ask for what you need.

Leviticus

Living as though you belong to God

I will turn my face to you, will make you fruitful and numerous, and will keep my covenant with you. You will still be eating the previous year's harvest when the time will come to clear it out to make room for the new! I will place my dwelling among you, and I will not despise you. I will walk around among you; I will be your God, and you will be my people. I am the LORD your God, who brought you out of Egypt's land—who brought you out from being Egypt's slaves. I broke your bonds and made you stand up straight.

Leviticus 26:9-13

Praying the word

As you read this scripture from Leviticus, say it out loud as a confession of God's promised presence. Then read it again, and let this passage remind you of times when God rescued you from large and small captivities. Are there places in your life where God's face seems turned away from you? Where would you want to see God "walk around" in your life this week? Picture a place where you work or play, and imagine that you and all those around you are intensely aware of your status as children of God. What does it look like in your imagination for God to dwell among you?

17

# Numbers

Blessings

The LORD bless you and protect you.
The LORD make his face shine on you and be gracious to you.
The LORD lift up his face to you and grant you peace.

Numbers 6:24-26

Praying the word

Where in your life do you need peace? In a relationship, a situation at work, or a decision you must make? Read these verses from Numbers as a prayer for your life. Turn over to God whatever is holding you back from the peace God desires for you. Be specific with God. Spend some time in silence as you name your need and as you give God thanks for hearing your prayer.

Deuteronomy

The way to well-being

Know then today and keep in mind that the LORD is the only God in heaven above or on earth below. There is no other. Keep the Lord's regulations and his commandments. I'm commanding them to you today for your well-being and for the well-being of your children after you, so that you may extend your time on the fertile land that the LORD your God is giving you forever.

Deuteronomy 4:39-40

Praying the word

Slowly read these words from Deuteronomy. When you are finished, read them a second time, listening and watching for one phrase of scripture that catches your attention today. This may be two or three words or a whole sentence. Go back to that one phrase and repeat it several times in a prayerful manner. Ask, "God, what do you want me to hear?" Spend time with this question and with what comes to mind for you.

☖ Joshua

Challenge to be faithful

*So now, revere the L*ORD*. Serve him honestly and faithfully. Put aside the gods that your ancestors served beyond the Euphrates and in Egypt and serve the L*ORD*. But if it seems wrong in your opinion to serve the L*ORD*, then choose today whom you will serve. Choose the gods whom your ancestors served beyond the Euphrates or the gods of the Amorites in whose land you live. But my family and I will serve the L*ORD*.*

Joshua 24:14-15

Praying the word

After reading these verses from Joshua, consider the "gods" in your life that distract you from placing God first. Don't rush past this question, but allow a time of prayerful confession to take shape from this text. We all serve other gods from day to day, but until we recognize and name them, we may be unable to make more room in our lives to serve the Lord our God. Pray that God may help you grow in faithfulness.

Judges

Now Deborah, a prophet

Now Deborah, a prophet, the wife of Lappidoth, was a leader of Israel at that time. She would sit under Deborah's palm tree between Ramah and Bethel in the Ephraim highlands, and the Israelites would come to her to settle disputes.

Judges 4:4-5

Praying the word

Who in your life or community is a wise person? Whom do you or others seek out for guidance, fairness, and reassurance? Have you had such people in your life before? What qualities and spiritual gifts did they offer? Create a prayer of gratitude for these people, giving God thanks for placing them on your path.

Ruth

Wherever you go

But Ruth replied [to Naomi], "Don't urge me to abandon you, to turn back from following after you. Wherever you go, I will go; and wherever you stay, I will stay. Your people will be my people, and your God will be my God."

Ruth 1:16

Praying the word

Reflect on this past week and on its events and activities. As you do, think of the people you spent time with. Allow time to recall each day, where you were, and who was with you. Now prayerfully consider who in these past days needed *you* to be with them. Whether this was for a few minutes or a few hours, whom did you spend time with this week who really needed you to be present with them? Remember how your presence was significant to that person, and thank God for allowing you to take that time for the ministry of presence. Hold that person in God's light for a few more moments.

1 Samuel

Samuel's call

A third time the LORD called Samuel. He got up, went to Eli, and said, "I'm here. You called me?"

Then Eli realized that it was the LORD who was calling the boy. So Eli said to Samuel, "Go and lie down. If he calls you, say, 'Speak, LORD. Your servant is listening.'" So Samuel went and lay down where he'd been.

Then the LORD came and stood there, calling just as before, "Samuel, Samuel!"

Samuel said, "Speak. Your servant is listening."

1 Samuel 3:8-10

Praying the word

Read through these verses about Samuel's call from God. It may be helpful to read it a few times, focusing on Samuel's phrase "Speak. Your servant is listening." Allow these words to become your breath prayer for this day. A breath prayer is simply a short prayer you can repeat off and on through the day; a prayer as close to you as breath; a prayer you can say with an inhale or an exhale; a prayer you can easily repeat over and over. "Speak. Your servant is listening. Speak. Your servant is listening." And then, quietly, listen for what God may be saying to you.

2 Samuel

My cry for help

[David] said:
>   The LORD is my solid rock, my fortress, my rescuer.
>   My God is my rock—I take refuge in him!—
>   he's my shield and my salvation's strength,
>   my place of safety and my shelter.
>   My savior! Save me from violence! . . .
> In my distress I cried out to the LORD;
>   I cried out to my God.
> God heard my voice from his temple;
>   my cry for help reached his ears.

2 Samuel 22:2-3, 7

Praying the word

Allow these words from 2 Samuel to reinforce for you that God hears your cries. For what in your life do you need to cry out to God today? How do you need God's help? What weighs heavily on your spirit? Offer a prayer to God that gives voice to your cry, to your longing, and to any distress you may be carrying. Trust that God hears you.

1 Kings

The Lord is passing by.

The LORD said, "Go out and stand at the mountain before the LORD. The LORD is passing by." A very strong wind tore through the mountains and broke apart the stones before the LORD. But the LORD wasn't in the wind. After the wind, there was an earthquake. But the LORD wasn't in the earthquake. After the earthquake, there was a fire. But the LORD wasn't in the fire. After the fire, there was a sound. Thin. Quiet. When Elijah heard it, he wrapped his face in his coat. He went out and stood at the cave's entrance. A voice came to him and said, "Why are you here, Elijah?"

1 Kings 19:11-13

Praying the word

Before you read this passage from 1 Kings, take a few moments to settle into the place you will be for this prayer time. Get comfortable, make the space as quiet as you can, and take a few deep breaths as you prepare to read. When you feel ready, read these verses slowly and prayerfully, allowing your imagination to help you see and feel the scene. What does God's presence feel like for you? When have you felt the presence of God? Let your memories of these times become your prayer, and ask God to help you grow in attentiveness and awareness of the divine presence.

△ 2 Kings

I won't leave you.

Now the LORD was going to take Elijah up to heaven in a windstorm, and Elijah and Elisha were leaving Gilgal. Elijah said to Elisha, "Stay here, because the LORD has sent me to Bethel."

But Elisha said, "As the LORD lives and as you live, I won't leave you." So they went down to Bethel. . . .

Elijah said, "Elisha, stay here, because the LORD has sent me to Jericho."

But Elisha said, "As the LORD lives and as you live, I won't leave you." So they went to Jericho. . . .

Elijah said to Elisha, "Stay here, because the LORD has sent me to the Jordan."

But Elisha said, "As the LORD lives and as you live, I won't leave you." So both of them went on together.

2 Kings 2:1-2, 4, 6

Praying the word

Read and reflect on these words about Elijah and Elisha, especially the words that Elisha repeats: "I won't leave you." Who in your life has been a constant, faithful presence, if only for a short season? How did that person let you know they were with you? Offer a prayer of gratitude for them. Now recall someone in your life for whom you have been a faithful presence. How have you reassured that person of your care? Is there someone who needs this from you now? Pray for that person as well, and for yourself, that you might be present to them.

1 Chronicles

David's song of praise

Give thanks to the LORD, call on his name;
make his deeds known to all people! . . .
The LORD—he is our God.
His justice is everywhere throughout the whole world.
God remembers his covenant forever,
the word he commanded to a thousand generations,
which he made with Abraham,
the solemn pledge he swore to Isaac. . . .
Bless the LORD, Israel's God,
from forever in the past to forever always.
And let all the people say, "Amen!"
Praise the LORD!

1 Chronicles 16:8, 14-16, 36

Praying the word

For what do you give thanks in your life today? Pause to review what you will be doing between now and the end of the day. Or, if you are reading this scripture in the evening, review this past day and all that you have done. What people, places, circumstances, and blessings did you encounter for which you can offer a prayer of thanksgiving to God? Create a simple prayer (for example, "God, I give you thanks for _____"), and lift up your gratitude to God for all that comes to mind.

2 Chronicles

Remembering a good place

The trumpeters and singers joined together to praise and thank the LORD as one. Accompanied by trumpets, cymbals, and other musical instruments, they began to sing, praising the LORD:

> *Yes, God is good!*
> *Yes, God's faithful love lasts forever!*

Then a cloud filled the LORD's temple. The priests were unable to carry out their duties on account of the cloud because the LORD's glory filled God's temple.

2 Chronicles 5:13-14

Praying the word

This reading describes a moment of worship during the dedication of Solomon's temple. For your prayer, reflect on ways that God has been good to you or to your family. If you can, think of a specific day or moment when you were convinced that God's faithful love would last a lifetime. Read the passage again, imagining that the trumpeters and singers are celebrating what God has done for you. Ask for an experience of God's glory powerful enough to interrupt your routine.

Ezra

Laying the foundation

When the builders laid the foundation of the LORD's temple, the priests clothed in their vests and carrying their trumpets, and the Levites the sons of Asaph with cymbals, arose to praise the LORD according to the directions of Israel's King David. They praised and gave thanks to the LORD, singing responsively, "He is good, his graciousness for Israel lasts forever."

All of the people shouted with praise to the LORD because the foundation of the LORD's house had been laid. But many of the older priests and Levites and heads of families, who had seen the first house, wept aloud when they saw the foundation of this house, although many others shouted loudly with joy. No one could distinguish the sound of the joyful shout from the sound of the people's weeping, because the people rejoiced very loudly. The sound was heard at a great distance.

Ezra 3:10-13

Praying the word

Take time to read this passage from Ezra slowly and thoughtfully. You may wish to read it more than once, using your imagination to re-create the sights, sounds, and emotions of the scene. Now focus on the image of the older members of the community weeping while others are joyful. For what, in your community, are the older members weeping? What causes them pain, suffering, and sadness? Offer a prayer to God for these people, for what breaks their hearts, for what causes them fear, and for what brings them to tears. Give God thanks for their lives, and ask God to bless and keep them.

Nehemiah

A God ready to forgive

You are a God ready to forgive, merciful and compassionate, very patient, and truly faithful.

Nehemiah 9:17c

Praying the word

Our prayers often reflect who God is for us, and in these prayerful words from Nehemiah, we read of a God who is forgiving, merciful, compassionate, patient, and faithful. When you pray, what are the qualities and attributes of God that shape your prayers? Comforting? Powerful? Forgiving? Near? Healing? Take time to reflect on who God is for you and on how you turn to God in prayer. Create a prayer, based on this reading, that uses four or five words to describe the God you perceive when you pray.

Esther

To help me be brave

Esther sent back this word to Mordecai: "Go, gather all the Jews who are in Susa and tell them to give up eating to help me be brave. They aren't to eat or drink anything for three whole days, and I myself will do the same, along with my female servants. Then, even though it's against the law, I will go to the king; and if I am to die, then die I will." So Mordecai left where he was and did exactly what Esther had ordered him.

Esther 4:15-17

Praying the word

Esther asks others to help her be brave in a time of trouble for her people. Her request is that they support her through the spiritual discipline of fasting, a form of prayer for many people. Where do you need to become more brave or courageous on behalf of other people? Are there circumstances in your life or in the lives of people you know or have heard about where the courage of others could be helpful? Offer God a prayer to help you find strength, courage, and wisdom on behalf of someone who needs your support.

Job

Establishing order

Then the LORD answered Job from the whirlwind: . . .
*   Where were you when I laid the earth's foundations?*
*   Tell me if you know.*
*   Who set its measurements? Surely you know.*
*   Who stretched a measuring tape on it?*
*   On what were its footings sunk;*
*   who laid its cornerstone,*
*   while the morning stars sang in unison*
*   and all the divine beings shouted?*
*   Who enclosed the Sea behind doors*
*   when it burst forth from the womb,*
*   when I made the clouds its garment,*
*   the dense clouds its wrap,*
*   when I imposed my limit for it,*
*   put on a bar and doors*
*   and said, "You may come this far, no farther;*
*   here your proud waves stop"?*

Job 38:1, 4-11

Praying the word

The grandeur of creation spans across our lives day by day, offering constant reminders that God is God, creator and redeemer of the universe. Sometimes our daily schedules are so busy and focused that we begin to live as though what we do is what keeps the universe running, but God will remind us otherwise if we will pay attention. Where— in creation or nature—do you experience the most awe? Is there an outdoor setting, a time of day, a favorite vacation place, a season of the year, or another natural reminder that helps you stay connected to God and to experience prayer in the moment? Spend a few moments of quiet as you recall where or when you experience prayer in creation. How do you feel when you are in that setting? How does that place draw you closer to God?

Psalms

Hope in God.

Make your ways known to me, LORD;
teach me your paths.
Lead me in your truth—teach it to me—
because you are the God who saves me.
I put my hope in you all day long.

Psalm 25:4-5

Praying the word

The psalmist wants to learn and to know God's ways, paths, and truth—to become a student or apprentice of God. Read this passage quietly a few times, and let it become your prayer as well. After the words become familiar, stop for a few minutes and identify a specific question in life for which you would like to have God's guidance. This may be about work, family, faith, a relationship, a decision, or a pending commitment. It can be anything you are feeling uncertain about or wanting God's help with to uncover some clarity for yourself. Now, with awareness of your particular need, pray the verses from the psalm again, connecting the prayer and your need. If you can, return to this prayer later in the day and week.

Proverbs

Wisdom

Doesn't Wisdom cry out
and Understanding shout?
Atop the heights along the path,
at the crossroads she takes her stand.
By the gate before the city, at the entrances she shouts:

I cry out to you, people;
my voice goes out to all of humanity. . . .
Take my instruction rather than silver,
knowledge rather than choice gold.
Wisdom is better than pearls;
nothing is more delightful than she. . . .
Now children, listen to me:
Happy are those who keep to my ways!
Listen to instruction, and be wise;
don't avoid it.
Happy are those who listen to me,
watching daily at my doors,
waiting at my doorposts.
Those who find me find life.

Proverbs 8:1-4, 10-11, 32-35a

Praying the word

After reading through these verses from Proverbs one time, pause in quiet. Then slowly read them again, watching for a word or phrase that catches your attention. Try to resist any analysis of the word or phrase so that even if it is small and at first insignificant, you will still allow yourself to attend to it. On a third reading of the text, stop at your word or phrase and repeat it to yourself several times. Stay with this part of the scripture, reflecting on what the word or phrase might mean for you this day. Spend a few prayerful minutes asking God why this word or phrase has stopped you and what God may want you to see or hear through it. Entrust to God any prayers that arise from this word or phrase for your life.

Ecclesiastes

All this is God's gift.

This is the one good thing I've seen: it's appropriate for people to eat, drink, and find enjoyment in all their hard work under the sun during the brief lifetime that God gives them because that's their lot in life. Also, whenever God gives people wealth and riches and enables them to enjoy it, to accept their place in the world and to find pleasure in their hard work—all this is God's gift. Indeed, people shouldn't brood too much over the days of their lives because God gives an answer in their hearts' joy.

Ecclesiastes 5:18-20

Praying the word

After reading this passage from Ecclesiastes, focus on a phrase that speaks to your life today. You may wish to read the full text a few times before making your choice. Once you have chosen, create a simple breath prayer (which you pray repeatedly) by adding to this phrase: "God, help me . . ." (for example, "God, help me find joy in hard work," or "enjoy your gifts," or "hear your answer when my heart is happy"). Take this prayer with you throughout this day.

Song of Songs

A refreshing well and restoring wind

You are a garden spring, a well of fresh water, streams from Lebanon.
Stir, north wind, and come, south wind!
Blow upon my garden; let its perfumes flow!
Song of Songs 4:15-16a

Praying the word

This passage is part of a call-and-response love poem where the lovers compare each other to a verdant garden with all its delights. Read this passage again and think of a desert place in your heart or story. How could the fresh water of God's love bring life to this parched place? What difference would it make to have God's wind at your back in this journey of faith? Close your eyes, and imagine a refreshing drink and a cool breeze as you use the first phrases from this passage today in prayer: "You are a garden spring. . . . Stir, north wind, and come, south wind!" Watch for subtle answers to this repeated prayer throughout the day.

 Isaiah

Seek the Lord.

Seek the LORD when he can still be found;
call him while he is yet near.
Let the wicked abandon their ways
and the sinful their schemes.
Let them return to the LORD so that he may have mercy on them,
to our God, because he is generous with forgiveness.
My plans aren't your plans,
nor are your ways my ways, says the LORD.
Just as the heavens are higher than the earth,
so are my ways higher than your ways,
and my plans than your plans.

Isaiah 55:6-9

Praying the word

Take time to reflect on news from the world, especially where there is conflict, cruelty, or suffering caused by human greed or lust for power. Allow this time of prayer to become a time of intercession for others in the world who have become victims at the hands of their neighbors. As you read these verses from Isaiah, pray that "the wicked abandon their ways and the sinful their schemes." Pray also that God's mercy will surround and embrace those who do harm, so much so that God's grace will transform their hearts. Ask God to help you to remember to pray for those who are suffering and for those who cause suffering.

Jeremiah

The time is coming.

The time is coming, declares the LORD, when I will make a new covenant with the people of Israel and Judah. It won't be like the covenant I made with their ancestors when I took them by the hand to lead them out of the land of Egypt. . . . No, this is the covenant that I will make with the people of Israel after that time, declares the LORD. I will put my Instructions within them and engrave them on their hearts.

Jeremiah 31:31-32a, 33b

Praying the word

What about God is engraved on your heart? Are there passages of scripture that you carry with you? Are there expectations or instructions that God has given to you and to others that you cherish and remember? As you read these words from Jeremiah about a new covenant between God and God's people, what are two or three instructions about faithful living that have deep significance for you and that you strive to follow? These might be, "Love the Lord your God," "Treat people in the same way that you want people to treat you," or "Pray continually." Choose for yourself, and once you have done so, allow these instructions to become your covenant prayer today.

Lamentations

Waiting for God

*Certainly the faithful love of the L*ORD *hasn't ended;*
certainly God's compassion isn't through!
They are renewed every morning. Great is your faithfulness.
*I think: The L*ORD *is my portion! Therefore, I'll wait for him.*
Lamentations 3:22-24

Praying the word

Read these verses from Lamentations at least two times, and do so slowly as you reflect on what the writer is trying to say to you—a reader in a new time and place. Receive these words as a direct offering to you from someone who shares your faith and love toward God. But also receive these words as a prayer for you, especially for something in your life about which you are being hard on yourself or self-critical. These words are urging you to be gentle and kind with yourself, as God is gentle and kind with you. Close your eyes and remember that God's love and compassion are always extended to you—no matter what has happened to shake your confidence. Know that the Lord is your portion and loves you always.

45

Ezekiel

A new heart

When I make myself holy among you in their sight, I will take you from the nations, I will gather you from all the countries, and I will bring you to your own fertile land. I will sprinkle clean water on you, and you will be cleansed of all your pollution. I will cleanse you of all your idols. I will give you a new heart and put a new spirit in you. I will remove your stony heart from your body and replace it with a living one.

Ezekiel 36:23c-26

Praying the word

At times our hearts harden. We become stubborn toward other people, different opinions and points of view, situations that make us uncomfortable, and even toward ourselves. After reading this scripture passage, sit quietly and reflect on the last time you felt your heart harden—or become "stony"—toward someone or something. What was happening at the time? Why did you respond with a stubborn heart? What would it take for your heart to soften again toward this person or circumstance? Offer a prayer that God might help your heart come alive again toward whatever caused your heart to become stony.

Daniel

Night vision

Daniel had a dream—a vision in his head as he lay on his bed. He wrote the dream down. Here is the beginning of the account:

I am Daniel. In the vision I had during the night I saw the four winds of heaven churning the great sea. . . .

As I continued to watch this night vision of mine,
I suddenly saw one like a human being coming with the heavenly clouds.
He came to the ancient one and was presented before him.
Rule, glory, and kingship were given to him;
all peoples, nations, and languages will serve him.
His rule is an everlasting one—it will never pass away!—
his kingship is indestructible.

Daniel 7:1b-2, 13-14

Praying the word

Begin by reading these verses from Daniel two or three times. Read slowly, taking time with each phrase and image. Try to put yourself in the place of the prophet, as though this were a dream you had. What do you see—colors, movement,

figures? What do you hear—crashing waves, wind?
What do you smell? Are there any tastes that come
to you as you reflect on this dream? Can you feel
anything against your skin? Go back to the text as you
live with each question, and allow your imagination
to enter the reading. Give God thanks for giving you
the gifts of imagination, sight, hearing, smell, taste, and
touch, through which you experience God's word in new
and prayerful ways.

Hosea

Divine promise of healing

I will heal their faithlessness; I will love them freely,
for my anger has turned from them. . . .
They will again live beneath my shadow,
they will flourish like a garden;
they will blossom like the vine.

Hosea 14:4, 7a

Praying the word

God's forgiving love is freely available to all people. These verses from Hosea remind us that this is true and that even when we have lived faithlessly, God is ready to restore our faith and to help us flourish again. Sometimes it's easier to accept this for others than for ourselves, but today's time of prayer is for you. Read and receive these words as God's message to you. Reflect on this past week, and wherever you haven't made faithful choices by something you did or neglected to do, release these behaviors to God. As our text says, God will love you freely and will heal your faithlessness. God's anger will turn from you, and God's love will surround you. Receive God's healing love today.

 Joel

Words of promise

I will pour out my spirit upon everyone;
*   your sons and your daughters will prophesy,*
*   your old men will dream dreams,*
*   and your young men will see visions.*

Joel 2:28

Praying the word

After reading these words from Joel, get into a comfortable position where you can remain for at least five minutes, if not more. Once you are comfortable, offer this prayer of petition over and over again, leaving space in between each repetition to listen for God's reply, however it may come to you. The prayer is, "God, please pour out your Holy Spirit upon me." That's all; just these words. Don't worry if you don't feel or experience a specific response to your prayer, but keep offering it with all your heart, mind, and strength: "God, please pour out your Holy Spirit upon me." After you have spent the time you can in prayer, close with "Amen," and trust that God has heard and responded to your petition.

Amos

A vision of a plumb line

The LORD said to me, "Amos, what do you see?"
"A plumb line," I said.
Then the LORD said,
"See, I am setting a plumb line in the middle of my people
*   Israel."*

Amos 7:8a

Praying the word

A plumb line is a tool used to determine whether a wall or beam is exactly upright (vertical). By setting a plumb line in the middle of the people, God's desire is to know how faithfully God's people are living according to the covenant they have with God. What helps you stay close to God's covenant? What keeps you in love with God and with neighbor? What helps you to love your enemies, to do justice, to love mercy, and to walk in humility? What makes you upright? Identify something specific in your life that helps your faith stay strong, and then write a prayer of gratitude and thanksgiving to God for what helps you to grow in faithfulness.

Obadiah

The cost of pride

Your proud heart has tricked you—
>   *you who live in the cracks of the rock,*
>   *whose dwelling is high above.*
> *You who say in your heart,*
>   *"Who will bring me down to the ground?"*
> *Though you soar like the eagle,*
>   *though your nest is set among the stars,*
>   *I will bring you down from there, says the LORD.*

Obadiah 1:3-4

Praying the word

When has pride come between you and someone you love? When has pride caused you to do harm or to lose your way? Read these two verses from Obadiah at least twice to get a sense of how pride damages the relationship between God and God's people. Then recall a time in your life when your own pride took a toll on your relationships with God and with others. Remember what was at stake for you and how pride "tricked" you into causing harm. Today offer a prayer to God to help you not be tempted or misled by pride as you grow in faithfulness to God's ways.

Jonah

Hearing God's word

*The L*ORD*'s word came to Jonah a second time: "Get up and go to Nineveh, that great city, and declare against it the proclamation that I am commanding you." And Jonah got up and went to Nineveh. . . . And he cried out, "Just forty days more and Nineveh will be overthrown!" And the people of Nineveh believed God. They proclaimed a fast and put on mourning clothes, from the greatest of them to the least significant.*

When word of it reached the king of Nineveh, he got up from his throne, stripped himself of his robe, covered himself with mourning clothes, and sat in ashes. Then he announced, ". . . Let humans and animals alike put on mourning clothes, and let them call upon God forcefully! And let all persons stop their evil behavior and the violence that's under their control!"

Jonah 3:1-3a, 4b-7a, 8

Praying the word

When God commands Jonah to go to Nineveh and proclaim what God tells him, Jonah listens and follows God's command. When the people of Nineveh hear Jonah speak, they believe he speaks for God, and they pay attention to his message.

When Nineveh's king is told about how his people believed Jonah and responded to Jonah's message, the king also believes that Jonah has heard from and speaks for God. This story from Jonah is built upon belief and trust in God and in God's word. If Jonah, the people, or Nineveh's king hadn't believed in God and in the power of God's word, we would have a different outcome. For your prayer today, ask for help listening for and believing in God's word—its power, its hope, and its light.

Micah

What does the Lord require?

He has told you, human one, what is good and
what the LORD requires from you:
> *to do justice, embrace faithful love, and walk humbly*
> *with your God.*

Micah 6:8

Praying the word

After reading the text from Micah, create a prayer using or paraphrasing the words from this passage. You might begin the prayer by naming people who need justice, faithful love, and humble hearts, and then ask God to help them. Or you could create a prayer of petition for God to help you act justly, love faithfully, and live more humbly. Take the instruction from Micah and create a prayer in any way you wish, but reflect on the significance of the words of the scripture as you do so.

Nahum

Power of the creator

> The Lord is very patient but great in power;
> > the Lord punishes.
> > His way is in whirlwind and storm;
> > > clouds are the dust of his feet.
> > He can blast the sea and make it dry up;
> > > he can dry up all the rivers. . . .
> > Who can stand before his indignation?
> > > Who can confront the heat of his fury?
> > > His wrath pours out like fire;
> > > > the rocks are shattered because of him.
> > The Lord is good, a haven in a day of distress.
> > > He acknowledges those who take refuge in him.
>
> **Nahum 1:3-4a, 6-7**

Praying the word

Read slowly through our scripture for today, noticing the many different ways in which the Lord is described here. Then read the passage a second time, making a list of all the attributes given to the Lord by the writer, such as patient, powerful, and punishing. Take your time, and use your imagination to list the many qualities inspired by this passage. Try to list at least ten, if not more. Then offer a prayer of praise and thanksgiving that God is God, the great I Am, full of mystery and power that are beyond our comprehension, and yet available to us where we are in any given circumstance.

Habakkuk

There is still a vision

I will take my post;
> *I will position myself on the fortress.*
> *I will keep watch to see what the Lord says to me*
> *and how he will respond to my complaint.*

Then the LORD answered me and said,
Write a vision, and make it plain upon a tablet so that a runner can read it.
> *There is still a vision for the appointed time;*
>> *it testifies to the end; it does not deceive.*
> *If it delays, wait for it;*
>> *for it is surely coming; it will not be late.*

Habakkuk 2:1-3

Praying the word

When you need to draw close to God, where do you "take your post"? Do you have a particular place that you can go to feel God's presence—a certain chair, a favorite view, a porch at dawn, or a lakeside at dusk? And is there a posture or position that helps you pray? Some find that lying on the ground, sitting on the floor, or walking outside helps deepen experiences of prayer. For today's prayer time, use this passage from Habakkuk to consider your "post" and "position" of prayer. Read the passage at least twice, and then reflect on your own prayer space and posture, being open to trying something different today and this week. Sit quietly in prayer as you consider new possibilities.

Zephaniah

Restoration

> The LORD your God is in your midst—a warrior bringing
> victory.
> He will create calm with his love;
> he will rejoice over you with singing.
>
> ### *Zephaniah 3:17*

Praying the word

After reading these words from Zephaniah, ask this question: "Where do I need calmness?" Allow yourself to review the past twenty-four hours in your life—conversations, meetings, errands, work, and family. Recall how you spent your time and how you felt throughout the day and evening—especially where there was tension, conflict, or stress. If there are any lingering issues from yesterday that still weigh on you today, pray that God would "create calm" for you. Invite God's loving calmness to be present to you throughout the rest of this day, especially in relation to issues from yesterday.

Haggai

The Lord's message

Then Haggai, the LORD*'s messenger, gave the* LORD*'s message*
to the people:
I am with you, says the LORD.

Haggai 1:13

Praying the word

This text from Haggai will become our breath prayer for today. For a few moments, simply repeat to yourself over and over again the phrase "I am with you, says the LORD." This may feel awkward at first, but give yourself permission to keep repeating it until you find a rhythm of prayer with these words. You may want to take time to consider the meaning of each separate word as you repeat the phrase, for each word carries its own significance. Memorize this prayer phrase, and after you have lived with it for several minutes, take it with you into your day, repeating it off and on whenever it comes to mind, even as you go to bed tonight. This is a prayer for your life.

Zechariah

Faithful decisions

The LORD of heavenly forces proclaims:

Make just and faithful decisions; show kindness and compassion to each other! Don't oppress the widow, the orphan, the stranger, and the poor; don't plan evil against each other!

Zechariah 7:9-10

Praying the word

By using the text from today's reading, begin with a prayer of petition: "God of my life, help me to make just and faithful decisions today. Amen." If it's helpful to pray this prayer a few times in order to settle into a prayerful posture, feel free to do so. Then take time to recall a specific decision that you're facing. Perhaps it is a decision about a family member or a coworker, or one about something you must either agree or decline to do. The decision can be anything in your life that requires your response. As you sit in prayer, allow time to review the decision and what is at stake for you and for others. Pray for God's help to stay faithful as you choose the way forward.

Malachi

The Lord whom you are seeking

Look, I am sending my messenger who will clear the path
*   before me;*
*   suddenly the LORD whom you are seeking will come to*
*   his temple.*
*   The messenger of the covenant in whom you take*
*   delight is coming,*
*   says the LORD of heavenly forces.*
Who can endure the day of his coming?
*   Who can withstand his appearance?*
He is like the refiner's fire or the cleaner's soap.

Malachi 3:1-2

Praying the word

Take time to get into a comfortable position for reading this passage in Malachi. Once you're ready, read the whole passage through one time. After a minute of silence, read it a second time, and as you do so, listen for a word or phrase from the reading that catches your attention. Resist second-guessing your choice, no matter what it is. During the next minute, quietly repeat your word or phrase to yourself. Then, as you read the text a third time, reflect on how your life is touched by this scripture passage. What do the verses cause you to think about? After three minutes of silent reflection, read the text one last time, asking, "Is there an invitation here for me to take action in some way?" Spend another few minutes in prayer, and see if the reading prompts any action or response from you that can be taken in the near future. Then close with "Amen."

Matthew

Happy people

Happy are people who are hungry and thirsty for righteousness, because they will be fed until they are full.

Happy are people who show mercy, because they will receive mercy.

Happy are people who have pure hearts, because they will see God.

Matthew 5:6-8

Praying the word

Who in your life "hungers for righteousness"? In all your relationship circles—family, friends, work, community—who fits the meaning of this phrase for you? Name this person. Whom do you know who shows mercy to others? Again, take time to recall people in your life who represent the meaning of this beatitude. Finally, do the same for someone who has a "pure heart." What does that mean to you, and how does this person's heart show through their actions or witness? Offer a prayer of thanksgiving for these people in your life.

△ Mark

God's kingdom

[Jesus] continued, "What's a good image for God's kingdom? What parable can I use to explain it? Consider a mustard seed. When scattered on the ground, it's the smallest of all the seeds on the earth; but when it's planted, it grows and becomes the largest of all vegetable plants. It produces such large branches that the birds in the sky are able to nest in its shade."

Mark 4:30-32

Praying the word

Imagine God giving you a mustard seed of faith to plant in your life. Close your eyes if it helps you really "see" this gift from God. What does this tiny seed look like in your hand? What does it feel like? You hold something precious to God and can do what you choose with this gift. What does the seed represent to you this day? Peace? Hope? Justice? Kindness? Love? Forgiveness? What do you most need this seed to grow into so that you can help God's kingdom come on earth as in heaven? Let this be your prayer.

Luke

Loving your neighbor

A legal expert stood up to test Jesus. "Teacher," he said, "what must I do to gain eternal life?"

Jesus replied, "What is written in the Law? How do you interpret it?"

He responded, "You must love the Lord your God with all your heart, with all your being, with all your strength, and with all your mind, and love your neighbor as yourself."

Jesus said to him, "You have answered correctly. Do this and you will live."

Luke 10:25-28

Praying the word

Read these verses from the Gospel of Luke, and then write down these six words: *heart, being, strength, mind, neighbor,* and *self.* For your prayer today, take time with each of these elements of the greatest commandment, first reflecting on what it means for you to love God with your heart. What does heart-love for God feel like? What evidence do you see in your life when you love God with all your heart? Then do the same prayerful reflection with the other five words. Let your prayer arise from your reflections, drawing you more deeply into the meaning of Jesus' words.

John

The story of the Word

In the beginning was the Word
and the Word was with God
and the Word was God.
The Word was with God in the beginning.
Everything came into being through the Word,
and without the Word
nothing came into being.
What came into being
through the Word was life,
and the life was the light for all people.

John 1:1-4

Praying the word

It may be that this scripture passage from John's Gospel is so familiar to you that it can be taken for granted. But today you are asked to read it prayerfully from a very personal perspective. Taking the last phrase, revise it slightly to read: "And the life was the light for me and for those I love." In other words, consider what it means that you and your loved ones are a significant part of "all people." Now reread the passage with intentional inclusion of yourself, because God has included you from your beginning. Prayerfully go from verse to verse, remembering that this is a word for your life: that you and the ones you love are held in God's life-light and always have been. For this word, give God thanks.

 Acts

God isn't far away.

In fact, God isn't far away from any of us. In God we live, move, and exist.

Acts 17:27b-28a

Praying the word

After reading this brief text from the book of Acts, sit in silent prayer and recall any people you know who are struggling to feel connected to God. Are there people who feel as though God has abandoned them or as though God is silent toward them? Are there others who feel let down by God or who simply feel that God is absent from their lives? Offer a prayer of intercession for each person who comes to mind. Lift each name into God's light of healing, comfort, and restoration. Pray for each one, placing them into God's loving presence. Throughout the day, remember these people when you can, and pray for them again and again.

Romans

The Spirit pleads our case.

We were saved in hope. If we see what we hope for, that isn't hope. Who hopes for what they already see? But if we hope for what we don't see, we wait for it with patience.

In the same way, the Spirit comes to help our weakness. We don't know what we should pray, but the Spirit himself pleads our case with unexpressed groans. The one who searches hearts knows how the Spirit thinks, because he pleads for the saints, consistent with God's will.

Romans 8:24-27

Praying the word

Take time to read these verses from Romans at least twice. If you desire, read the passage a few more times until you feel centered in it. When you have completed your reading, ask this question: "What is my hope for the people of God?" When you think about all that is going on in the world today, where can hope make a difference? What do you hope for most deeply? How does hope influence your faith? Let this time of prayer be about hope—what it is for you, what it is for others, and what it represents to you about God. Wait in hope.

1 Corinthians

Love

If I speak in tongues of human beings and of angels but I don't have love, I'm a clanging gong or a clashing cymbal. If I have the gift of prophecy and I know all the mysteries and everything else, and if I have such complete faith that I can move mountains but I don't have love, I'm nothing. If I give away everything that I have and hand over my own body to feel good about what I've done but I don't have love, I receive no benefit whatsoever.

1 Corinthians 13:1-3

Praying the word

Without love, the rest of our gifts and talents can't be fulfilled. Our reading from 1 Corinthians reminds us of this principle. No matter what else we have to offer others, if we don't also extend love, our offers are incomplete. For today's time of prayer inspired by the reading, choose someone close to you who needs to know you love them. Once you have made your choice, plan to let this person know of your love before night falls. Even if you have already told this person today, make time to tell them again, because love is to be shared over and over again. Let your words of love become your prayer.

2 Corinthians

Written on the heart

You are our letter, written on our hearts, known and read by everyone. You show that you are Christ's letter, delivered by us. You weren't written with ink but with the Spirit of the living God. You weren't written on tablets of stone but on tablets of human hearts.

2 Corinthians 3:2-3

Praying the word

Slowly and prayerfully read these two verses from 2 Corinthians. Then in your imagination, or, if you prefer, on this page or on a piece of paper, write a brief letter about what it means to you to be a Christ-follower. What do you want others to know about God, Jesus Christ, and the Holy Spirit? What are you willing to share about what you believe? Why is your faith important? It may help to have a particular person or group in mind as you craft your letter, but let your words become your prayer of witness.

☖ Galatians

God's children

Because you are sons and daughters, God sent the Spirit of his Son into our hearts, crying, "Abba, Father!" Therefore, you are no longer a slave but a son or daughter, and if you are his child, then you are also an heir through God.

Galatians 4:6-7

Praying the word

In God, you have a trustworthy parent. As God's daughter or son, you have full freedom to share any matter of your heart with the one who created you and who loves you unconditionally. Therefore, on this day, you are encouraged to share with God anything that burdens your heart, especially things that you feel you can't share with anyone else. Practice trust with your prayers today, revealing whatever may be gnawing or tugging at your conscience or consciousness. Come to God in prayer as a child who is loved completely, no matter what, by your Parent, who is always ready to hear you and to embrace you in grace. In silent prayer, share with God what is on your heart.

Ephesians

Saved by God's grace

You are saved by God's grace because of your faith. This salvation is God's gift. It's not something you possessed. It's not something you did that you can be proud of. Instead, we are God's accomplishment, created in Christ Jesus to do good things. God planned for these good things to be the way that we live our lives.

Ephesians 2:8-10

Praying the word

Begin today's prayer time by silently reading through the passage from Ephesians to get a feel for the whole text. When you have finished, pause for a minute, and then prepare to read it again. As you read, watch for a word or phrase in the text that catches your attention. Remember, any word or phrase will do, whether short or long. Repeat this word or phrase to yourself quietly for another minute, letting it make a home in you. Now read the full passage a third time, but begin by asking, "How does this scripture touch my life?" As you read, use this question as a compass, and pay attention for any connection to your life that comes to mind. Spend two or three minutes with this connection. Finally, prepare to read the passage one final time, using the question "Is there an invitation from this scripture for me?" As you read the words from Ephesians, be open to any prompting or invitation that may come to you, especially one that you can act on in the near future. Close with "Amen."

Philippians

God will be with you.

From now on, brothers and sisters, if anything is excellent and if anything is admirable, focus your thoughts on these things: all that is true, all that is holy, all that is just, all that is pure, all that is lovely, and all that is worthy of praise. Practice these things: whatever you learned, received, heard, or saw in us. The God of peace will be with you.

Philippians 4:8-9

Praying the word

Today in prayer, focus on "these things" that are listed in the scripture: "all that is true, all that is holy, all that is just, all that is pure, all that is lovely, and all that is worthy of praise." Taking each of these phrases one at a time, reflect on one thing or person in your life whom the words describe. What is one truth for you? What is something holy for you? What in your life is just? What is pure? What or who is lovely? What or who is worthy of praise? Don't hurry through these reflections, but when you are finished, give God thanks for all that comes to mind.

Colossians

The peace of Christ

Therefore, as God's choice, holy and loved, put on compassion, kindness, humility, gentleness, and patience. Be tolerant with each other and, if someone has a complaint against anyone, forgive each other. As the Lord forgave you, so also forgive each other. And over all these things put on love, which is the perfect bond of unity. The peace of Christ must control your hearts—a peace into which you were called in one body. And be thankful people.

Colossians 3:12-15

Praying the word

Read these verses from Colossians at least twice, becoming reacquainted with the qualities of the Christian life listed here. In the next twenty-four hours, how might each of these qualities become part of your "clothing"? Consider the activities and interactions you will or could have today, and reflect on how you can "wear" compassion, kindness, humility, gentleness, patience, tolerance, and forgiveness. Notice the text doesn't suggest that one of these qualities is chosen, but that all of them are available for you to "put on." Pray that God will help you this day, and give God thanks for the peace of Christ that you will share with others.

1 Thessalonians

Rejoice always.

Rejoice always. Pray continually. Give thanks in every situation because this is God's will for you in Christ Jesus. Don't suppress the Spirit.

1 Thessalonians 5:16-19

Praying the word

Review the past day and night—what you did, where you went, with whom you spent time—and create a list on this page or on another piece of paper. Begin with when you first awoke to begin your day, and continue through when you went to bed. After making your list, go back to each item that you included and examine how you can be grateful for each event—even if, on first review, it wasn't a "good" experience. How can gratitude still enter into "every situation" from yesterday? Offer God a prayer of gratitude for guiding you through yesterday and for being with you today and every day to come.

2 Thessalonians

God chose you.

But we always must thank God for you, brothers and sisters who are loved by God. This is because he chose you from the beginning to be the first crop of the harvest. This brought salvation, through your dedication to God by the Spirit and through your belief in the truth. God called all of you through our good news so you could posses the honor of our Lord Jesus Christ.

2 Thessalonians 2:13-14

Praying the word

These verses from 2 Thessalonians are part of a letter written to a faith community to remind them that they are loved. Who in your life needs to hear this from you? Is there a friend, family member, or acquaintance who can use this word of encouragement and affirmation from you? Let this be your prayer today: that you will take time to write, call, or visit someone this week to simply tell them you are grateful for them and they are loved. In your prayer today, spend time praying for other people in your life, and choose at least one to be in touch with this week.

1 Timothy

Our hope is set.

This saying is reliable and deserves complete acceptance. We work and struggle for this: "Our hope is set on the living God, who is the savior of all people, especially those who believe."

1 Timothy 4:9-10

Praying the word

From these few words in 1 Timothy comes a breath prayer for today. You may wish to change or paraphrase these words to better fit your prayer, but begin with something like this: "My hope is set on you, God," or "God, you are my hope. I believe." Again, a breath prayer needs to be very short and very personal, so take time with the essence of this scripture passage, and create a prayer that you can use from memory throughout the day and week. Once you have your prayer, spend several minutes quietly repeating your prayer over and over again, allowing the prayer to find a rhythm with your breathing in and out. Try to use this prayer off and on through the upcoming days.

2 Timothy

A holy calling

God is the one who saved and called us with a holy calling. This wasn't based on what we have done, but it was based on his own purpose and grace that he gave us in Christ Jesus before time began.

2 Timothy 1:9

Praying the word

When does helping someone else bring you joy? What kind of work or service nourishes your spirit? Are there talents or abilities you have that make you feel energized and whole when you are using them? Sometimes these inner feelings are evidence of living out a "holy calling." God has created all people to contribute to and to participate in the fullness and restoration of creation through our gifts and capacities to love God and neighbor. By using this passage from 2 Timothy as encouragement, identify one gift, ability, or purpose you believe God has given you to use in the world, and ask God to help you continue to be faithful with this gift.

Titus

Inherit the hope.

We were once foolish, disobedient, deceived, and slaves to our desires and various pleasures too. We were spending our lives in evil behavior and jealousy. We were disgusting, and we hated other people. But "when God our savior's kindness and love appeared, he saved us because of his mercy, not because of righteous things we had done. He did it through the washing of new birth and the renewing by the Holy Spirit, which God poured out upon us generously through Jesus Christ our savior. So, since we have been made righteous by his grace, we can inherit the hope for eternal life."

Titus 3:3-7

Praying the word

Read these verses from Titus two or three times, going slowly so that you can take in the whole passage. For today's prayer time, use this reading as a guide to a prayer of confession and mercy. First, consider how deception or jealousy is present in your life right now. Are you keeping the truth from or feeling jealous of someone in your life, even in a small way? If neither of these behaviors fits, take time to identify what else might be keeping you from full commitment to God. Once you have named your confession to God, pray, "Lord, in your mercy, hear my prayer. Christ, in your mercy, hear my prayer. Lord, in your mercy, hear my prayer. Amen." Release to God your jealousy, deception, or other burden, and go in peace.

Philemon

Radically redefined relationships

Maybe this is the reason that Onesimus was separated from you for a while so that you might have him back forever—no longer as a slave but more than a slave—that is, as a dearly loved brother. He is especially a dearly loved brother to me. How much more can he become a brother to you, personally and spiritually in the Lord!

Philemon 1:15-16

Praying the word

Paul's short letter to his "dearly loved coworker," Philemon, on behalf of a runaway slave named Onesimus, is very personal. Thoughtful readers find that this particular story offers an opportunity for rethinking their most broken relationships. Paul suggests that maybe the separation of Philemon and Onesimus has occurred so their relationship can be radically redefined by Jesus Christ. Is there someone in your life with whom you have a strained or even a hostile relationship? Has someone hurt or betrayed you? Using these verses as a guide, pray, "God, help me see _____ (name) no longer as a _____, but more than a _____—as a dearly loved sister/brother." Then pray for someone else in this situation ("God, help them see _____ as a dearly loved sister/brother").

Hebrews

The imprint of God's being

In the past, God spoke through the prophets to our ancestors in many times and many ways. In these final days, though, he spoke to us through a Son. God made his Son the heir of everything and created the world through him. The Son is the light of God's glory and the imprint of God's being.

Hebrews 1:1-3a

Praying the word

Slowly read this passage from Hebrews, spending time with each phrase. As you read the last sentence, center on the word *imprint*. Use your imagination to recall different imprints you have seen. What is left behind in an imprint? What does an imprint reveal? This scripture reminds us in beautiful language about who Jesus Christ is and about what the incarnation reveals about God. In your prayer time, simply reread these verses slowly and quietly, again taking time with the image given that the Son is the imprint of God's being. May God be revealed to you this day as you remember the life, death, and resurrection of the living Christ, who calls you to follow him.

James

Courageous patience

Therefore, brothers and sisters, you must be patient as you wait for the coming of the Lord. Consider the farmer who waits patiently for the coming of rain in the fall and spring, looking forward to the precious fruit of the earth. You also must wait patiently, strengthening your resolve, because the coming of the Lord is near. Don't complain about each other, brothers and sisters, so that you won't be judged. Look! The judge is standing at the door!

James 5:7-9

Praying the word

Recall a time in your life when you had to wait patiently for something important to take place. Be specific as you choose one season or event where patience was required and where you had to practice ways to wait and live patiently. Write down what you remember—when this was, what was happening, where you lived, who was involved. Once you have done this, try to remember what helped you to be patient—worship, friends, exercise, prayer, music? What activities or practices supported you as you waited patiently? As you read this passage from James, consider how God might help you to grow in patience as a practice of faith, and let this be your prayer: that God would grant you the patience to live more faithfully.

1 Peter

God's life-giving word

As you set yourselves apart by your obedience to the truth so that you might have genuine affection for your fellow believers, love each other deeply and earnestly. Do this because you have been given new birth—not from the type of seed that decays but from seed that doesn't. This seed is God's life-giving and enduring word.

1 Peter 1:22-23

Praying the word

Read through these two verses from 1 Peter, then pause for a minute of silent reflection before you read them again. Upon completion of the second reading, return to the words "genuine affection for your fellow believers, love each other deeply and earnestly." For this time of prayer, identify someone you know who is a "fellow believer" but whose beliefs don't agree with yours in some way. You may not see eye-to-eye about holy scripture, a church issue, a congregational decision, or an interpretation of faith with your brother or sister in Christ. Offer a prayer for this person and for yourself, asking God to help you have "genuine affection" and deep love for them in spite of your different perspectives. Live with this prayer through the week.

2 Peter

God's promise

Don't let it escape your notice, dear friends, that with the Lord a single day is like a thousand years and a thousand years are like a single day. The Lord isn't slow to keep his promise, as some think of slowness, but he is patient toward you, not wanting anyone to perish but all to change their hearts and lives.

2 Peter 3:8-9

Praying the word

Our reading assures us that God waits patiently for us to grow and to change as people of faith. God meets us where we are but also reveals to us how our hearts and lives need to change to fully become the people God creates us to be. In what ways do your heart and life need to change to follow Jesus more faithfully? What do you long for from God? What do you long to offer God through your life? May your prayer today be a prayer of petition that God will help you change your heart in a way that deepens your faith.

1 John

The message: God is light.

This is the message that we have heard from him and announce to you: "God is light and there is no darkness in him at all." If we claim, "We have fellowship with him," and live in the darkness, we are lying and do not act truthfully. But if we live in the light in the same way as he is in the light, we have fellowship with each other, and the blood of Jesus, his Son, cleanses us from every sin.

1 John 1:5-7

Praying the word

After reading the scripture passage assigned for today, focus on the imagery used about light and darkness. Intercessory prayer will be your practice today, guided by the scripture. First, think of news from around the world or from your region or neighborhood, and recall where there are people living in "dark" and heavy circumstances. This may be under the threat of war, hunger, human trafficking, addiction, loneliness, incarceration, poverty, genocide, job loss, or other circumstances brought on by human conflict, neglect, or hunger for power. For each circumstance that comes to mind, pray,

"God, let your light shine in that place." If, at the end of this time of prayer, one particular situation stays with you, learn more about it this week and continue to pray for light to reveal what is happening to the people there.

2 John

Love each other.

Now, dear friends, I am requesting that we love each other. It's not as though I'm writing a new command to you, but it's one we have had from the beginning. This is love: that we live according to his commands. This is the command that you heard from the beginning: live in love.

2 John 1:5-6

Praying the word

Read the selected verses from 2 John two or three times, appreciating their simplicity and clarity regarding the great command we have from God in Christ Jesus: live in love. This is your prayer today: live in love. To carry it with you, open the hand that you don't write with, and, with the other hand, use a finger to "write" these words in the palm of your hand: *live in love.* Or, if you prefer, just imagine these words being written on your heart. Take this prayer with you from this day forward.

3 John

Imitate what is good.

Don't imitate what is bad but what is good. Whoever practices what is good belongs to God. Whoever practices what is bad has not seen God.

3 John 1:11

Praying the word

Whom do you know whose faith has qualities you would like to imitate? Name one person, and write down what it is about this person's faith that you admire or are drawn to. Take prayerful time to recall how this person's faith is made evident, or what it is about them that is attractive to you. What "good practices" would be worth imitating? After you have spent time in reflection, offer a prayer of thanksgiving for this person in your life. If it feels right to you later in the week, consider letting this person know that they set an example of faithfulness for you.

Jude

A strategy for the faithful

Build each other up on the foundation of your most holy faith, pray in the Holy Spirit, keep each other in the love of God, wait for the mercy of our Lord Jesus Christ, who will give you eternal life. Have mercy on those who doubt.

Jude 1:20b-22

Praying the word

After a first reading of this passage from Jude, read the words a second time, listening for a word or phrase in the passage that claims your attention. As before, try to resist analyzing or second-guessing your word or phrase, no matter how small or long it may be. Trust that this is the word or phrase God needs you to see. For a few minutes, softly repeat your word or phrase several times, staying open to what thoughts or experiences it brings to mind. Now prepare to read the scripture a third time with this question before you: "How does this scripture touch my life?" Read the passage and see what stirs in you after three or four minutes of silent reflection. When ready, read the passage a fourth time, asking, "Is there an invitation here for me?" Take some closing time in prayer

94

to see if you feel pulled toward a response or an action by your word, phrase, or by the scripture. Pray that God will help you live out the invitation and response that you have received.

Revelation

Jesus is coming soon.

Look! I'm coming soon. My reward is with me, to repay all people as their actions deserve. I am the alpha and the omega, the first and the last, the beginning and the end. . . .

I, Jesus, have sent my angel to bear witness to all of you about these things for the churches. I'm the root and descendant of David, the bright morning star. The Spirit and the bride say, "Come!" Let the one who hears say, "Come!" And let the one who is thirsty come! Let the one who wishes receive life-giving water as a gift.

Revelation 22:12-13, 16-17

Praying the word

Go slowly as you read these verses from Revelation. Read them aloud at least one time through, listening to each word as you pronounce it. Pray that you are "one who hears" what Jesus is saying to you. "Come!" Pray your response to Christ's invitation to come and drink of the living water for which you and all people thirst. "Come!" Let your prayer today be, "Come, Lord Jesus, quickly come," and carry this prayer with you into the hours and days ahead, especially when you sense your thirst for the life-giving water of God.